PASSPORT TO THE FUTURE

By Rinus Le Roux

COPYRIGHT AND PUBLISHING

CONTENTS

ABOUT THE AUTHOR

Rinus le Roux is a professional speaker, trainer and author.

His life is dedicated to the development of human potential.

He observes, contemplates and comments on human behaviour and how to improve it.

You are welcome to contact me at: rinus@ucan.co.za

Become part of your PASSPPORT TO THE FUTURE and visit: **www.ucan.co.za**

FOREWORD

The future belongs to those who choose to live more from the heart than from the head. In "Passport to the Future" you may just find a few clues as to how to do that. - *Archbishop Emeritus Desmond Tutu*

DEDICATION

To André You touched my life in the most amazing way and gave meaning to my future when I needed it most. *- Yoroshii -*

INTRODUCTION

This passport is for those who choose a positive future – for those individuals who choose to be driven by hope and possibility and NOT by fear and impossibility.

AS A CITIZEN OF THE SOVEREIGN REPUBLIC OF SIGNIFICANCE, YOU HAVE

VOW NEVER TO BE FOOLED AGAIN

'You're human if you are fooled once, but you're a fool if you are fooled twice'

Whether it was a politician, an evangelist, a salesman or even that shrewd fat kid across the street who conned you out of your lunch, we've all been fooled at one time or another.

To be fooled means that someone or some group makes you believe something that it is in their interests for you to believe, rather than in your own. An example is the TV evangelist who tells you that if you don't give a thousand dollars towards his new jet plane you will not be blessed. So you fork out the money in order to receive the blessing when the truth is that all he wants is to fly in luxury.

I know people who have been subjected to a lifetime of being taken for a ride. They have chosen to follow blindly, rather than question and think for themselves, and thus have missed out on personal growth.

We so often sacrifice our future and the wonderful opportunities for growth and learning that this offers because we remain in a 'fooled' state.

I want to encourage you to look at your life and make sure that you are not trapped in a 'fooled' state by some person or group with vested interests that have nothing to do with your own. In doing so, you will embark on a future of self-reliance and develop the confidence to trust your own instincts and logical faculties when confronted with choices designed by others to take advantage of you.

THE RISK OF TAKING THE 'CHICKEN RUN'

At the airport many years ago, while saying goodbye to friends who had decided to leave the country, I could only think of one thing to say to them: 'Wherever you go, you take yourself with you.'

The type of people who are irritating you now, will irritate you wherever you go. Traffic jams will get to you wherever you drive. Crime, as low as the rate might be at your destination, does not discriminate. Frustration with government will become an issue again in whichever country you choose to live. The truth is that discontent lies not without; it lies within.

It is everyone's right to choose to leave but, before you take this decision, take some time to search your heart and befriend the person you see in the mirror. Come to terms with all those nagging flaws you experience in your daily life because they go where you go.

Finally, there is one more issue to consider:

Where is it that you feel you should rather be?

Strange question, perhaps, but one that is worth asking. If you feel that it is your calling to help solve conflict or to uplift the less fortunate, perhaps you are already in precisely the place you are supposed to be. If, on the other hand, it is your life's purpose to study polar bears in Antarctica, that is a separate matter and this might not be the place for you.

If you can find peace in your heart and come to terms with these issues, you will know what to do and your heart will lead you to where you are needed.

'If you believe in oneness, there is really no geographical location that will give you peace. You will have to find peace within first.'

SLAYING THE WOLF AT THE FOOT OF THE BED

'Some of us will face our fears and destroy them. Some of us will be destroyed by them and some of us will forever have to fight them.'

There is a wolf that I need to warn you about. Many of you may have seen him only once or twice and some of you have never seen him at all, but for others he is a constant reality. He lies at the foot of your bed and, while looking you straight in the eye, he divulges your future second by second.

This wolf preys on fear, anxiety and depression.

Sometimes he can be vicious and tear your heart apart with fear; at other times he can disable you with his eyes and sap your energy in the form of depression. Sometimes he can stare you down and show his teeth, paralysing you with anxiety. This wolf will not only steal your future but swallow it whole while you look on helpless and disabled.

I wish there was a sure way to advise you as to how to destroy this wolf. For some meditation is a must while for others physical activity and a good diet help. Sometimes the confession of our deepest sins or quiet hours of contemplation and meditation set us free. Most of the time it is a combination of a variety of mental, physical and spiritual remedies that will keep the wolf at bay.

A friendly warning: If you are serious about your future, fight this wolf or he will destroy your future.

NEVER LET A GOOD CRISIS PASS YOU BY

'You may have to wait a while before you have another crisis, so capitalise on this one.'

Most of you reading this book will inevitably go through yet another tough economic crisis as experienced by the world in 2009/2010. The question is: What have you

learned from this one?

Well-known personality Clem Sunter mentioned this topic in one of his speeches, prompting me to investigate it.

The great thing about a crisis is that it presents you with very rare opportunities. You may have to wait a long time before these opportunities are presented to you again.

Here are a number of valuable things that came out of the recession for me:

- I learned to value my existing customers.
- It sharpened my networking and sales skills.

- I revisited some 'left behind' markets.
- I learned that panicking doesn't help.
- I became fit.
- I learned to express appreciation.

Any crisis presents multiple opportunities of which most include learning and development, but crises also offer many tangible opportunities to streamline your business or ways of doing business in order to increase customer service levels, cut unnecessary costs, and many more.

Similarly, a crisis in one's personal life is rich in opportunities for growth and development. It could prompt you to take stock of whom and what you are, to evaluate what is really important to you, and help you to refocus on your goals or set new ones.

LET THE LEADERS LEAD OR LET THEM LEAVE

'We deserve our leaders and their leadership because we have elected them. So, next time, think before you make the 7.'

To this you may say, 'I didn't elect them' and that you need someone else in power.

Instead of constantly criticising, you need to get with the program.

- Stand for local government or in your own area.
- If not, have a discussion with the leadership in your ward.
- Start a pressure group and start to lobby for your rights.
- Have those difficult conversations and start creating awareness
- Write down what you want from your leaders and push to get it.
- Write articles for your local newspaper and become an opinion leader.

There are many things you can do to fix leadership. The worst thing you can do is to say 'it won't work' or 'we are up against too much' or 'we are too small a minority group' or any other negative sentiment you care to name.

Our world is in desperate need of great leaders – people who are willing to assume this position and, more than this, who are able to lead with both head and heart.

Imagine how Martin Luther King Jr, Nelson Mandela, Mahatma Gandhi, Che Guevara and many others leaders of their ilk would respond to you. Remember that if you have to ask the question, 'Where are we going?' or 'What is the country (or world) coming to?' then you have just defined yourself as a follower and not a leader.

FINE TUNE YOUR PHYSICAL VEHICLE

'The less broken and the better tuned your physical vehicle is, the greater your chances of survival on a planet that selects the fittes and wisest.'

By a fine-tuned vehicle I literally mean the energy you can summon on a daily basis to conquer your future. This therefore doesn't necessarily refer to the physical fitness of the guy at the gym with the greatest biceps or the most defined abs. Nor does it refer to the intellectual fitness of the academic in his ivory tower who neglects his health in favour of the life of the mind. In fact, I know many disabled people whose drive and energy levels exceed those of so called 'able' people.

This vehicle is the most important tool you have on Planet

Earth. Without it, there is no future for you on this planet.

From my point of view, the most critical issue is your levels of energy. These levels, as you know, are determined by:

- the quality of your food and drink
- the daily exercise you do
- the state of your mind
- the energy you deplete through fear and worry.
- the energy you absorb by exposing yourself to
- beauty, love and gratitude, and the extent of your
- concern for the wellbeing of others
- quiet moments of meditation

You can still blast into the future with a vehicle with no doors, a broken speedometer and worn-out seats, but you can't get there without any fuel.

BE A 'TEN'

'To abandon the lower levels, more dense energy, which is tainted with negativity, and move to higher, more positive energy, we need to constantly be mindful that it is a choice.'

A well-dressed man walks into a convenience store, ostensibly to pick up a French loaf of bread. He stands around with the bread, looking for a paper bag.

He sees a shop assistant and lets rip, telling her how terrible the store and the service is, and how she doesn't even deserve to be paid at the end of the month because of the non-availability of brown

paper bags. **Behaviour – 1.**

Same story, but this time the man tells the shop assistant that there are no paper bags available at the bread counter and, with a smile, asks her to please fetch him one. He then offers to recommend her for a bonus for her good service.

Behaviour – 10.
This is not about service; it is about behaviour.

We all know the difference between 1 and 10 behaviour. We are all able spot it, even when blindfolded. I don't know about you, but I would love to live in a world where '10' behaviour is the norm rather than '1' behaviour.

No person, family or nation wakes up one morning to find that there has been a shift from 1 to 10 behaviour overnight. Behaviour takes practice and with practice come the trials and tests to establish whether one's behaviour has really changed. But it is a fact that you need to start by being mindful and choosing '10' behaviour. You then need to start encouraging and rewarding '10' behaviour when you see evidence of this in others.

Before hosting the Olympic Games in Seoul, South Korea, citizens were encouraged to practise good behaviour. They had designated days of kindness, days of giving way to motorists, and they even

learned to queue properly. We all know that when the Olympics was hosted by Beijing, China, people stopped spitting in public because other nations find it offensive. Behaviour that is practised becomes habit.

Practice '10' behaviour and soon youwill be known as a '10'.

BECOME FEEDBACK FIT

- Strongly Agree
- Agree
- Neutral
- Disagree
- Strongly Disagree

'Allow feedback to inspire you rather than destroy you.'

If you can succeed in not taking feedback too personally, you will do well. When you are praised, look at it with the same analytical eye as when you are criticised. This will give you the opportunity to grow from both praise and criticism.

If you focus on a better future, all feedback will be to your benefit as you can utilise it to achieve this end.

We tend to take some feedback more seriously than the rest. For example, if someone we respect and idolise gives us feedback, we take it much more personally than when it comes from someone we don't really know or don't necessarily have that much respect for.

In both instances make sure that you understand what the feedback is all about. If you can, ask a question or two to determine what the person giving the feedback really means. This will give you the opportunity to make real adjustments to your perspective, output or behaviour rather than simply speculating on what the feedback truly was about.

Remember, most importantly, that you can make of the

feedback whatever you want. Once given to you, it is
yours to evaluate, internalise or reject – the choice is yours.

The more advanced we become, the more we will welcome feedback and use it to our advantage in

the future.

WHAT GOT US HERE WON'T GET US ANY FURTHER

'If you look at our world and see the need for change, you will know that the tools, concepts and ways of doing that got us thus far will not get us any further.'

The left brainers with their MBAs, blue suits, red ties, zero people skills and 'know it all' attitudes have had their chances and screwed up for long enough. The textbook models work on paper but the problem is that we don't live and work on paper.

The fear-based religions with evangelists screaming at the top of their lungs that Lucifer is on the loose have reached their sell-by date.

The economic plans that make the rich richer, the poor poorer and the arrogant unbearable have served their term and failed us.

Maybe it's time we stopped tying the Windsor knot around our necks, using the Queen's English in our oh-so-boring PowerPoint presentations and loosened up a bit.

Maybe it's time to chuck out a few old habits, lose the stiffness of our colonial mannerisms and start operating to make a difference.

There is no need for countless meetings and the formal adoption of a bill in order to feed hungry children and to take care of business.

It took a hell of a lot of growing pains and unnecessary red tape and red faces to get us here. The time has come to allow the free thinkers, the creative problem solvers with right-brain capacity, to take charge and get us further.

CREATE THE FUTURE BEFORE YOU GET THERE

'I can see my future. Can you see yours?'

Is the future truly a space where there are endless opportunities waiting to be defined and taken up by us as we arrive? If so, it makes perfect sense to be one step ahead – to create the future before we get there.

When we revisit Einstein's theory, we see that time and space are irrelevant. That means that if we create images of the future right now in the present, we are in fact becoming co-creators of our future. If we believe that 'as we think so shall we be', we are able to link 'as' (present) and 'be' (future) in our minds. In other words, if we start creating these images in our minds, we are already beginning to manifest them in the future.

Those who read and understood *The Secret* and *The Law of Attraction* will know that we start co-creating the future in the present.

The clearer and the more detailed our vision of the future the better our chances of arriving at the future with what we envisaged in mind. By 'detailed'

I mean fine detail such as colour, smell, timelines, geographical areas, emotions … The more detailed the images we conjure up the better.

If you have a dream for the future, make sure that you can visualise that dream in sharp focus, vivid multicolour, 3D and surround sound, right here and now in the present.

GIVING UP IS NOT AN OPTION

'The problem with giving up is that if you give up today, what are you going to do tomorrow? Give up again ...?'

If you are old enough to read this, you are old enough to have had the desire to give up. Yes, just to stop doing anything and give up!

It was on a Tuesday in the late afternoon that my biggest client called to tell me they'd sent me an email

I should read immediately. On doing so I discovered that this client was experiencing financial difficulty and had therefore cancelled my contract. Within the next 48 hours I had received further bad news and by Friday morning I was physically, mentally and most definitely financially stressed out.

I therefore cancelled the meetings I had scheduled for Saturday and for Monday of the following week.

By Monday morning I was ready to flat-line. I wanted to give up. In fact, I had already taken the mental and physical decision to give up. I slept the whole day, tossed and turned throughout the night, and by early Tuesday morning I had again decided to give up on my career. Since drowning myself in the bath or jumping off a building is not really an option for me, all I can tell you is that for a whole week in my life, I had totally given up hope. The question then was: What do I do next?

The answer was actually very simple. The future does not allow you to give up. It only allows you to rest, pick yourself up, seek help, get motivated and move on. In some respects it is scary to realise that whether you give up or not, the next second, minute, hour, day and week will still be there. Yet, seen in a positive light, this means that you are already part of the future.

It is up to you to re-align, revitalise, reenergise and put yourself in a position to seize the opportunities the next moment of your life can potentially offer you.

The past is the past but the future offers infinite possibilities.

HAVE A MIND OF A CAPITALIST AND THE HEART OF A SOCIALIST

'The secret of our economic future lies in finding the balance between the welfare of the needy and the aspirations of the greedy'

I know of a strange planet where food and drink are available in abundance. A small percentage of people buy and sell the produce and make millions from it. On the same planet millions of people die from of hunger and malnutrition. Strange planet, wouldn't you say? I suspect it must be a Godforsaken place.

To all the capitalists screaming 'crucify him', and the socialists screaming 'saint him', hang on ...

This is not a question of choosing one economic system over the other; it is a question of balance. The problem is that the 'haves' are not nearly as willing as the 'have nots' to explore the balance, which is understandable if you operate from a perspective of scarcity.

It is the capitalist who sees opportunities, who has the guts to take risks, put deals together, negotiate great terms and bring his or her vision to fruition and gestalt. It goes without saying that for this spirit of entrepreneurship, risk-taking and tenacity there must be an above-average reward.

On the other side of the coin are the people who execute the dreams and plans of the entrepreneurs and risk takers. These are the people who devote their care, energy and skills to making the vision a reality. These people need to be taken care of too.

Within any economic system there are casualties who have been chewed up and spat out by the system. They too need to be taken care of in some way. Face it. You cannot own a mansion in the middle of a war zone and expect to sleep well at night.

The key is balance!

HAVE FUN

'They say the reason why angels can fly is because they take themselves lightly.'

The future is layered with endless opportunities. It is a clean slate ready for us to colour in and give form to. What a wonderful opportunity to fill it with fun and laughter! The more we experience the lighter side of life, the more positive endorphins will be released by our bodies and the better our experience of life will be.

Commit yourself to at least one fun activity per day.

If you are not sure what to do, consider the following:

- Seek some sunshine.
- Change the voicemail greeting on your cell phone daily.
- Hug or kiss someone you love.
- Take random photos with your cell phone and share them.
- Eat something fresh and natural.
- Walk naked in your home.
- Eat with your hands.
- Go for a wee outside (mostly men).
- Take a different route home or to work.

It is not what you do; it is the mindset that counts. It is the willingness to enter the future with a smile and not to let anything wipe that smile off your face.

I might not be able to guarantee you a longer life if you have more fun, but I can guarantee you a 'lighter' and more stress-free life if you choose to have more fun.

INVEST IN THE BRAND ME

'Investing in your brand is an investment in your future. You owe it to yourself to develop and refine your brand.'

Brand strategists all over the globe are paid very good money to look after the big brands of the world. They work with brand identity, the values that the brand stands for, how the brand is represented in printed and electronic media and in the hundreds of other applications of the brand.

Furthermore, on a daily basis, individuals travel to offices and pay to work for and with these top brands so that we can learn to recognise them and choose to make themour preferred brands.

This is all good and well, but the question is: What do you do to develop and maintain your personal brand?

Have you spent sufficient time on determining your own brand identity? Are you operating from a specific set of values and are you serious about your own personal development?

Think about it. The words you speak, the people you associate and don't associate with, the clothes you wear, the way you carry yourself – all of these determine your personal brand.

You invest a lot of energy, time, ability and money in building the brands you work for, but it is even more important to become serious about investing these same resources in building personal brand value.

To be competitive in the future, you will have to make a continual investment in your own brand.

THE RULES OF ENGAGEMENT - COMMON DECENCY

At times I wonder whether the majority of the population missed out on attending kindergarten.

In my case, most of the basic rules of engagement that apply in life at any age I learned from my beautiful kindergarten teacher who, when she smiled, lit up my life and made me feel as if I was the most important person in the class – in itself a powerful rule of engagement.

For those who missed the basics, allow me to recap a few of the fundamentals that will make your future blossom. These are the absolute basics without which we simply cannot get by:

- Say hello and goodbye.
- Say 'please' and 'thank you' when you ask for something.
- Never take anything that doesn't belong to you.
- Respect all people and especially older people.
- If you wonder whether it is your turn to take out
- the trash, take it out anyway.
- Praise often and criticise constructively.
- Make eye contact and smile.

Here are a few more advanced rules of engagement:

- When speaking to someone, give that person your full attention.
- Don't always better someone's story with your own.
- Ask questions about people's lives and show an interest in them.
- When you've made a mistake, be big enough to admit it and ask for forgiveness.
- Respect the values, beliefs and traditions of other people.
- When shaking hands, bowing or giving someone a hug, make sure you leave a trace of your physical and spiritual energy behind to be remembered by.
- Make sure no one leaves your home hungry, thirsty or insulted.

The more perceptive we become, the higher our consciousness will rise and the better we will understand how to use the rules of engagement to create a better future.

'Most of the things we need to know about common decency we learned at kindergarten.'

I AM BECAUSE OF YOU

'In the absence of that which I am not, that which I am cannot exist'

If the wizard of truth came to me and told me I could choose one truth to give to mankind, this is the one

I would choose. Whether you test it from a religious, philosophical, agnostic, humanitarian or any other point of view, it remains true and powerful.

Let's test it in two ways: Religious: In the absence of that which I am not (God), that which I am (Rinus) cannot exist. Philosophical: In the absence of that which I am not (a woman), that which I am (a man) cannot exist.

By now you've figured out that this truth deals, to some extent, with dualism. Therefore in the absence of everything you are not, it is impossible for everything you are to exist. To take it a step further, everything exists only because its polar opposite also exists. In the absence of the one, the other is devoid of meaning.

If you can truly embrace this concept, you will be able to comprehend that this planet, with all of its duality, exists in order for us to learn about who we are not and to experience and to grow in who we are. This also provides us with the choice to change. If you are a negative person, this negativity cannot exist unless there are others with a positive attitude. At the risk of complicating even further this already complex philosophical truth, it is potentially possible for you to change your attitude from negative to positive and thereby to become, in relation to those with a negative attitude, the opposite of what you were originally.

At the risk of belabouring this point, consider further:

- Black and white people can only know and identify themselves as such because of the existence of each other.
- Kind people can only experience themselves as kind because of the presence of the unkind.
- In the absence of suffering we cannot experience bliss.

If you think about it, this phenomenal way of approaching life makes perfect sense and could well constitute the ideal formula for a better life based on insight into the nature of polar opposites and the inextricable relationship between them.

COMMIT RANDOM ACTS OF KINDNESS

'Isn't it wonderful that our deepest experience of significance occurs when we give without any expectation of being rewarded?'

Perhaps the reason we struggle to unconditionally give of ourselves, our money and our possessions is our default setting founded on the false belief that there is not enough for everyone on this planet. We therefore feel that we constantly need to collect and hold back as much as we can.

One doesn't need to research the topic of scarcity extensively to find out that this myth does not come from a shortage of resources but rather from the greed of those who have access to these resources.

This phenomenon has developed not only with regard to physical resources but includes emotional and spiritual resources as well.

Some of the false beliefs that surround the myth of scarcity are the following: Being too friendly can be seen as a weakness, so rather don't be friendly at all.

Being kind can result in people taking advantage of your kindness. Having a giving nature might result in being left with nothing and finding nobody willing to give to you.

The truth is that when we give – be it of ourselves, our money or our possessions – we truly experience our significance through these acts. We all know the power of a smile, a kind word, a pat on the back, or words of appreciation.

Most of these gestures require a good attitude and don't cost a thing. These random acts of kindness prove that we are more than physical beings – that we are, in the true sense of the word, spiritual beings.

A key principle to manifest a prosperous future is to practise these random acts of kindness in the present without expectation of reward.

HAVE THOSE DIFFICULT CONVERSATIONS

'The more uncomfortable the conversation, the greater the opportunity to discover new frontiers and deeper meanings.'

A few weeks before my sixteenth birthday, I found a new book on my bed entitled *What Every Boy Should Know*. After dinner, my dad told me to read it and to ask him if I had any questions. This was the extent of my sex education.

We all tend to avoid these difficult conversations about sex, religion, politics, race, death, illness, betrayal, etc because we don't know how to conduct them. Yet the fact is that the quality of our future and our personal development depends largely on our willingness to discuss these controversial and difficult issues. They provide us with insight into ourselves and others, and open up a whole new realm of possibilities for us.

At the risk of simplifying this very valuable tool to uncover the future, there are a few ground rules:

- Take the decision to switch roles. Consider taking on the other person's argument while he or she takes on yours.

- Detach from any outcome. Argue the point, not for the sake of winning or losing, but to explore another point of view.
- Respect your point of view but, more importantly, respect the other person's point of view.
- Leave your ego out of the equation; don't be self-centred.
- Focus on the opportunity to break new ground and impact on the future.
- Know that to see another point of view doesn't mean betraying your own beliefs, values or principles. It simply means exploring opportunities to create a better future.

As an avid advocate of Popular Narrative Psychology, I think the best chance we have

of cracking open the treasures of the future is

through engaging in difficult conversations.

WHEN YOU PASS THE TEST IN THE PRESENT YOU PROGRESS TO A BETTER FUTURE

"This is Earth School. We come here to learn, to play, to grow...and this is possible in both "good" times and "not so good" times.'

Consider, for a moment, that you enter this world as an infant with only the most basic survival instincts. How, then, do you get to know things? You learn!

When it comes to the really important virtues in life such as patience, forgiveness, compassion, love, selflessness, self-reliance and many more, you need to learn those too. Not from a textbook or a lecture, but through practical experience. In the same way, you are never going to get into shape, no matter how many books on fitness you have on your bookshelves, unless you make time to do physical exercise.

If you want to learn the virtue of patience, one way is through getting stuck in traffic when you are in a hurry.

Or you might just find that the answers you seek are not coming your way quickly enough. This too teaches you to be patient.

A more difficult virtue (lesson) to learn may be forgiveness. How can you ever learn to forgive if no one has ever wronged you? Take the time to think about all of those occasions in your life when someone has done you harm or hurt your feelings. These are the people you called to teach you forgiveness.

This is Earth School. We come here to learn, but we cannot be taught unless we are willing to learn. I am your teacher and you are mine.

EARTH - PRESERVE HER

'Perhaps when the last tree falls and we gasp for oxygen, perhaps then we will know this planet was our future.'

There are many things for which we are granted an extension, such as paying our taxes and our TV licenses, removing the rubble from the pavements, rescheduling an appointment with the dentist, and soon. But the one thing we cannot postpone is caring for our planet. Face it. We have nowhere else to go.

We all know by now that this planet is not healthy. The symptoms range from global warming to polluted water, swine flu, bird flu, tsunamis, earthquakes, floods and many other catastrophic disasters.

It may seem to you as if one person cannot make a difference and, without the participation of others, this perception is correct. But when we extend this to include you and me and all of us together, we can most definitely make a difference. Apart from what we can do in our individual households (eg recycling our rubbish, conserving energy and water), we can also join pressure groups to force governments and large corporates to be much more responsible in preserving our planet.

If we don't heed this call right now Greenpeace's message 'We told you so ...' will have a tragic ring in time to come because by then it will be too late.

All the elements in this book directed at creating a better future depend 100 per cent on the continued wellbeing of a planet called Earth. Without her we

are not.

THE MASTER ALCHEMIST

'The ancient alchemist could transform lead into gold. The master alchemist can transform negative energy into positive energy.'

During the 11th century the 'magic' practice of alchemy was developed. The alchemist was said to have the knowledge and skills to put lead through a tempering process and thereby transform it into gold – a much sought-after craft as you can imagine.

This skill thus becomes a metaphor for the ability to transform something considered not intrinsically precious into something very precious, or negatives into positives. The key concept is the ability to transform.

Every time one of us encounters a negative situation or a negative person and we take on the challenge of transforming that situation or person into something positive, we are practising alchemy.

The master alchemist looks for every possible opportunity to change the negative, useless stuff into positive, meaningful stuff. For this to happen, the alchemist (you) will have to:

- Be willing to get involved. To experience total quality of life you cannot sit on the sidelines. The alchemist must constantly be willing to get involved in situations where these golden moments can be created.

- Express yourself. The world needs you to express your talents, your skills and your abilities. When you do this with the positive power, not only do you benefit, but we all benefit because of you. These golden moments and the future wealth they create in all spheres of life depend on your willingness to practise alchemy.

THE QUALITY OF YOUR LIFE DEPENDS LARGELY ON THE QUALITY OF THE QUESTIONS YOU ARE WILLING TO ASK

'The only reasons we don't ask the quality questions is because we fear the quality answers.'

Most of us come from a background where it is expected of us to accept what we've been told and not to question. Although this is definitely changing, the art of asking quality questions still needs some mastering.

'Do you love me?' is a good question but, if given the opportunity, one could ask a few follow-up questions that

would get you closer to the truth. For example: 'Are you going to stay with me?' 'What bothers you about me?' 'Is your love linked to any conditions?' 'Will you be able to forgive me?'

So, when you ask someone, 'Do you love me?' you must be clear on what it is you really and truly want to know and ask questions related to the real issue.

The crux of this topic is to find the deeper yes and the deeper no in order to unlock greater opportunities and to overcome large obstacles as early as possible before they seem too big to overcome.

Think about your family, country, the planet, etc and come up with those deeper questions that will unlock the greater issues and opportunities. The key is to work through a hierarchy of questions, beginning with those that are less revealing and progressing to the more penetrating, more sharply focused quality questions and, more importantly, those quality answers.

THE FUTURE OF WORK

'The secret is to work because you want to, not because you have to. The one is driven by passion, the other by fear.'

If the quality of the future economy depends o the happiness of the workforce, I suspect the world is in trouble. I continually hear people complaining about work – how they can't stand what they do or who they are managed by.

If you are working a forty-hour week you are spending roughly 25% of your life at work. This doesn't include the time you spend thinking about work, or driving to and from work. If you feel unfulfilled in your work, you cannot afford to waste such a large slice of your life in a state unhappiness and dissatisfaction, lacking meaningful purpose and hindering your personal development. Work is supposed to be an

opportunity to demonstrate your skills, to interact and to grow.

For a very long time the world has been concerned about work/life balance and rightfully so, but the responsibility has now shifted to you, the employee, to pace yourself and to blend your working life and your personal life experience into a quality of life experience.

In some cultures the concept of retirement does not even exist and I often hear of people who are just sitting it out in their jobs, waiting for retirement.

How about not wanting ever to retire? What if we can find a vocation that creates so much meaning for us that we want to continue doing it for as long as we possibly can?

For us to find work/life balance, to work for as long as we can, to enjoy work, we will have to change our perceptions of work. We are not paying for our sins when we work. In fact, we are creating a meaningful and significant future for ourselves, our families and the world in general.

If you love what you do, you won't have to work another day in your life.

WE ARE GOVERNED BY OUR HIGHTEST VALUES

In the final analysis it seems that we are not really true to our ideals or promises or even to each other. We are truest to our highest values.'

The society and social structure in which I grew up was fairly rigid; order and compliance were two very important values.

The school I attended had strict rules regarding length of hair, the wearing of nail polish, waiting in line and moving from one classroom to another in silence. We obeyed the rules of the government and attended an orderly church.

Compare this type of life with that of a child who has to queue for a taxi, arrives at school late because of transport problems, is against the government and takes part in protest marches, and who has to rally and shout loudly in order to get a point across.

Without taking sides and not without sympathy, compare the value systems of these two individuals.

The one will stop at traffic lights, speak when spoken to, and adhere to the values of orderliness and respect. The other would tend to do almost the

exact opposite. For us to adhere to government's rules and regulations, we need to be able to align our value systems with these. Over and above these prescribed rules, it is our values that dictate to us what is right and what is wrong.

A friend of mine from the USA married a traditional African woman who comes from a strong ethnic background with close ties to the customs and values of her tribe. My friend was born and raised with the American values of liberty, freedom of expression and opportunity.

Can you feel the potential friction regarding differing value systems in this case?

Please note, for instance, that if someone values freedom very highly, this doesn't mean that they don't have family values. It simply means that one value is higher in priority than another and we mostly honour our highest values. The hierarchy of these values keep changing with time as we grow and develop. For example, what is high on the hierarchy when you are single might occupy a much lower position once you have a family.

When we interact with people they almost immediately give us clues about their value

system and so do we. It is very powerful to observe and compare these in order to move forward with our friendships and relationships.

This is true in both our personal and business lives. Most important is to use this information, not to judge, but rather to understand and fosterbetter interaction in the future.

THE FUTURE BELONGS TO THOSE WHO ARE WILLING TO DEFINE THEIR PURPOSE

'The more defined and refined your purpose, the brighter and better your future will be.'

The question 'What is my purpose?' has always felt a little too difficult and even a bit rhetorical to me. Perhaps the question should rather be: 'What do I do, or how do I get involved in a way that creates purpose in my life?'

For me the essence of purpose is not to know it but to live it. Knowing it and not living it will create huge frustration within you and will eventually result in a feeling of wasted time, wasted opportunities and a wasted life.

Important questions to ask yourself will be:

- What makes me feel alive and excited when I do it?
- Which projects do I get enthusiastic about?

- What is it that makes me look forward to another day?
- Where do I feel I add value and make a difference?

Whether you choose to be a monk, sell your possessions and go on a spiritual journey, be a spokesperson for animal rights, work at a convenience store, climb the corporate ladder and be an executive, or any other vocation you may choose, the important question is this:

While pursuing your vocation, do you feel meaningful, significant and enthusiastic?

If you do, you are busy living your purpose and will continue creating opportunities in the future to do more of it. If you don't, you need to set out on a journey of discovery and to allow yourself to get involved in projects where you may find your bliss.

The advantage is that the more certain you become about what makes you feel excited, enthusiastic and significant, the easier it becomes to enter the future with purpose.

THANK GOD FOR E=MC2

Newton said if the apple falls from the tree, it will hit the ground – gravity!! Einstein said it might not, as someone may catch the apple before it hits the ground – relativity!!"

In a world where we thought the laws of physic were cast in stone and in the true sense of the word "laws" we found out that this all is relative. Time, space, etc. is relative to Einstein and his followers.

What this means in the world of meta-physics (beyond physics) is that all our thoughts, experiences and perceptions are relative – that the observer determines that what is being observed.

And how does this impact the future? Well, the rules, the morals, the goal posts, the ethics will keep changing in the future. Relax, this doesn't mean you have to sacrifice your core to survive in the future.

It means that what you thought was static in the past might not be that static in the future.

You as the observer might have to be willing to change your point of view and be willing to accommodate people with different points of view.

Be willing to stay open and let go of ridged thought patterns and opinions and adopt a more fluent and liquid approach to life and the future.

A final thought – if everything is relative then nothing really matters, except the things such as kindness, love, giving and those non-concrete things in life.

SEE THE CONTEXT

'Nothing exists in isolation. Everything stands in context and in relation to everything else.'

A sure way to compromise the future is to have a single-minded approach to life. There is an obvious and, most of the time, not so obvious link between everything in life.

The truth is sacrificed when there is no context.

Think about the hunting habits of carnivores in the wild. When seen from the perspective of the hunted

- the elegant young gazelle with its helpless eyes
- the killing seems unnecessarily violent and cruel.

However, when seen from the perspective of the hunter – the lion that may not have eaten for weeks and is in desperate need of food for its cubs – one's sympathy could just as easily shift from the hunted to the hunter.

We often take sides when it comes to war, with one member of a couple going through a divorce, with people who hold similar values to our own, etc, but for us to really form an unbiased opinion it is important to see all events in context.

Context gives us the opportunity to form a more balanced and informed opinion. In South Africa, our national soccer team is rated 88th in the world, which is really not good, but our financial institutions are rated 5th in the world which is excellent. If you judge the country purely on the basis of the world rating of its national soccer team it might make you laugh until you look at the rating of its financial institutions. Add the crime rate and the picture changes again. Now look at poverty and compare with poverty in other countries (e.g. India) and the picture keeps changing. As you go through this exercise you keep broadening your focus as you as place these issues in context.

Wherever you go, whatever you see or experience, ask yourself whether you are seeing the situation in context. More importantly, admit to yourself that without a shadow of a doubt there are facts and issues that you are not aware of and therefore your opinion will be just that – your opinion. The more information and understanding you gain, the more context will influence that understanding and the more informed your opinion will be.

A MESSAGE FROM THE FUTURE

I am the FUTURE.

I am where you will soon arrive.

Contrary to what you may think, I hold nothing for you – no secrets, no sorrows, no pleasures. I am simply patiently awaiting your arrival.

All that will be, will be co-created by you and the Creator. What you believe or don't believe is no concern of mine. I don't judge you or your creations. The reason I am here is to present infinite opportunities for you to choose from.

It is fairly simple: you choose now in your present and you receive your present when you arrive here.

Until we meet, choose wisely and enjoy your present as you have chosen even this moment.

WHATEVER YOU KEEP IN YOUR MIND WILL EVENTUALLY BE SEEN ON YOUR FACE

No mind-reading skills are required to fathom what most people are thinking while sitting in a traffic jam. Their thoughts are written all over their faces.Imagine the expression these faces will wear after years of sitting in traffic jams!

At a park in my hometown I sat reading on a bench, watching a grandmother walking with her grandchildren, exploring the flowers, bees, bugs and butterflies. Her face lit up every time a child laughed and, momentarily, one could see a lifetime of beautiful and peaceful thoughts in her eyes and in her smile. The same type of expression I saw on the face of the Dalai Lama when I once attended a lecture presented by him.

Months ago I visited a friend's father who has been bedridden for several years. His eyes are tearful, he appears a little anxious and fear is written all over his 93-year-old face. He is afraid to be alone and the prospect of death petrifies him.

In these two instances I could see how that which you constantly keep in your mind will find an expression on your face. You may think that the frown on your forehead, the clenching of your jaw, or the squinting of your eyes is momentary, but it isn't. Your tendency to select and to dwell on the inconvenience, frustration and discontent that you experience at times will accompany you into the future and will eventually be the expression your family, friends and colleagues will see on your face for the rest of your life.

You know the saying: 'As we think, so shall we be.'

'Our bodies are an expression of our thoughts in visible form.'

YOUR RESPONSE TO THE STIMULI IN THE OUTER WORLD IS A REFLECTION OF THE STATE OF YOUR INNER WORLD

'All that you see and experience merely mirrors that which you hold within yourself.'

The following quote comes from the book Illusions, written by Richard Bach: 'The depth of your ignorance can be measured by your belief in injustice ...'

He implies that everything is simply the way it is and acquires a specific meaning only through the viewpoint of the observer. I guess that is where the expression 'the glass is half full/half empty' comes from. How it is described depends on whether the observer is an optimist or a pessimist.

There are numerous examples available to prove this point but it is still very hard to accept one's outer world is a reflection of one's inner world. Another story that illustrates this is about the two salesmen who that went to a rural area to sell shoes. The one came back claiming that there is no market as no one wears shoes there, while the other felt sure that there is a massive market because no one has shoes.

In the same way, one prisoner will see the bars on the window of his cell while another sees the stars.

This principle becomes somewhat more difficultwhen we look at some of the judgements we make:

- I can't stand stupid people.
- I hate people who gossip.
- Why don't poor people stop procreating?
- People who eat with their hands have no manners.
- My religion is the only one that is right.
- This is not culture, it is barbarism.
- If you want to work, you'll find a job.

- He/she is so disrespectful.

- The new generation has no work ethic.

  - I wish he would cut his hair.
  - They (people of a different race or culture) are all the same, etc.

The urge to justify these judgements on the basis that 'I know what I know and I can see what is right and what is wrong' is very normal at this point.

However, consider for a moment how a wise master might view these value judgements. He would be able to consider his own point of view in relation to those of others, knowing that there are many people out there who hold exactly the opposite view from his. So, how do we disengage sufficiently from our own opinions in order to be able to consider the variety of others that exist?

Think about an international sports match. When one team scores, some spectators are elated and some discouraged. The master is able to acknowledge good play from both sides. We are all at the mercy of different ongoing stimuli. What is important is how we choose to react to them.

It was Deepak Chopra who said that we are all part of the same hologram in which each individual piece represents the whole. So each one of us is representative of our total consciousness and reflects that.

When we look outside ourselves, we are literally seeing the reflection of ourselves and our own inner state – literally branches from the same tree, and there is no tree so stupid as to blame, judge or kill its own branches.